MW01010451

An Ideas Into Action Guidebook

How to Launch a Team

Start Right for Success

IDEAS INTO ACTION GUIDEBOOKS

Aimed at managers and executives who are concerned with their own and others' development, each guidebook in this series gives specific advice on how to complete a developmental task or solve a leadership problem.

LEAD CONTRIBUTORS	Kim Kanaga
	Sonya Prestridge
CONTRIBUTORS	Henry Browning
	Michael Kossler
GUIDEBOOK ADVISORY GROUP	Victoria A. Guthrie
	Cynthia D. McCauley
DIRECTOR OF PUBLICATIONS	Martin Wilcox
EDITOR	Peter Scisco
WRITER	Janet Fox
DESIGN AND LAYOUT	Joanne Ferguson
CONTRIBUTING ARTISTS	Laura J. Gibson
	Chris Wilson, 29 & Company

Copyright ©2002 Center for Creative Leadership.

All Rights Reserved. No part of this publication may be reproduced, stored in a retrieval system, or transmitted, in any form or by any means, electronic, mechanical, photocopying, recording, or otherwise, without the prior written permission of the publisher. Printed in the United States of America.

CCL No. 417
ISBN No. 1-882197-71-2

CENTER FOR CREATIVE LEADERSHIP
POST OFFICE BOX 26300
GREENSBORO, NORTH CAROLINA 27438-6300
336-288-7210
WWW.CCL.ORG/PUBLICATIONS

AN IDEAS INTO ACTION GUIDEBOOK

How to Launch a Team

Start Right for Success

Kim Kanaga and Sonya Prestridge

Center for
Creative
Leadership

NORTH AMERICA EUROPE ASIA

www.ccl.org

THE IDEAS INTO ACTION GUIDEBOOK SERIES

This series of guidebooks draws on the practical knowledge that the Center for Creative Leadership (CCL®) has generated in the course of more than thirty years of research and educational activity conducted in partnership with hundreds of thousands of managers and executives. Much of this knowledge is shared—in a way that is distinct from the typical university department, professional association, or consultancy. CCL is not simply a collection of individual experts, although the individual credentials of its staff are impressive; rather it is a community, with its members holding certain principles in common and working together to understand and generate practical responses to today's leadership and organizational challenges.

The purpose of the series is to provide managers with specific advice on how to complete a developmental task or solve a leadership challenge. In doing that, the series carries out CCL's mission to advance the understanding, practice, and development of leadership for the benefit of society worldwide. We think you will find the Ideas Into Action Guidebooks an important addition to your leadership toolkit.

Table of Contents

EXECUTIVE BRIEF

When an organization sponsors a team, it's usually to address a challenge deemed essential to organizational success. Meeting that challenge might mean implementing new ways of working, entering new markets, or developing a new product. Teams can produce innovative solutions, but leading them toward that goal can be difficult. Getting the team off on the right foot is critical to its success. To launch a team in a way that increases its chance of success, managers and team leaders should pay attention to four critical points: setting purpose and direction, defining roles and responsibilities, designing procedures and practices, and building cooperation and relationships. Understanding and implementing these elements is key to a successful launch and, in the end, essential to a team's achieving the organization's goals.

The Right Start Is Critical to Success

Teams are a popular approach to many business challenges. They can produce innovative solutions to complex problems, enabling organizations to be faster, more responsive, more competitive, and more successful in meeting their missions. But these kinds of results aren't guaranteed. It's not always easy for teams to deliver high performance, and the price of team failure can be very high. One of the first steps to take toward increasing team effectiveness is to pay attention to how the team is formed. You can head off most of the problems that beset teams during the formation stage by setting a clear direction, securing organizational support, selecting the right team members, building an enabling team design, developing key relations, and monitoring external factors.

Still, even if you have formed your team with those guidelines in mind, high performance isn't inevitable. A well-planned and orchestrated team launch is crucial to keeping your team moving toward success. Right from the beginning, team members have to know what their mission is, how success will be measured, and how they will work together. From the start they need to feel inspired by the opportunity to serve on a team, be confident that they will have the resources and support needed for success, and feel good about the people they will depend on to accomplish the team's mission.

The Center for Creative Leadership (CCL) has a long history of work with teams. In the course of that work it has become clear that four sets of activities spell the difference between a successful team launch and an unsuccessful one:

1. setting purpose and direction
2. defining roles and responsibilities

3. designing procedures and practices

4. building cooperation and relationships.

When you take on the responsibility of leading a team, you can launch your team toward success by addressing all of these elements.

Launching a Successful Team

The crucial business of a team launch is to *become* a team – to bring a group of disparate and formerly disconnected people with their varied skills and experience and styles to bear on a challenge. The actions you take as team leader before, during, and after the first team meeting – the time of the team's launch – will help your team achieve that first important step. Team members will learn why they have come together to make a team, get to know each other, begin to trust each other, and learn to work together outside of and across from their usual channels and boundaries. They will set up the terms of how they will interact with one another to achieve their shared purpose. Throughout this process you will lead your team in setting its purpose and direction, defining team member roles and responsibilities, settling on procedures, and building relationships.

When it comes to launching your team you may find that getting all the members together in one place poses a significant challenge. Many teams today are likely to be geographically dispersed, separated by time and distance. In preparing your team for launch, pay careful attention to the logistical challenge of getting your team together for its first meeting and, further, to coordinating additional meetings (especially if your team will be working together for six months or longer).

The Important First Meeting

The first team meeting should be face to face. It can be as long as 2–3 days or as short as 2–3 hours with a scheduled series of meetings to follow. The initial meeting should include all team members, the team leader, the high-level sponsor of the initiative, and perhaps a meeting facilitator. The agenda should include:

- discuss team purpose/charter
- discuss vision/mission/goals/timelines
- understand why each person is on the team
- understand processes of how work will get done
- get to know individuals and their roles
- work out team norms
- work out communication processes
- work out decision-making processes
- set up meeting documentation/minutes/records of key decisions.

After this first face-to-face meeting, distribute meeting minutes and descriptions of the processes and norms to which the team has agreed. Also send a schedule of future meetings to team members.

Videoconferencing and other communication technologies make it possible to hold meetings in which the participants work in a variety of locations. But CCL research suggests that the benefits of at least one initial face-to-face meeting are significant to reinforcing a team design that empowers its team members to take initiative, work together, and achieve team goals. The benefits of an initial face-to-face meeting include creating a sense of camaraderie that can't be produced by other forms of communication, laying the groundwork upon which team members can build trust (trust that will be needed to work through inevitable conflicts and to solve complex problems), and providing clarity about the team's goals.

Setting Purpose and Direction

What are we here to accomplish?

Research at CCL indicates that a lack of clarity about team purpose is a major cause of team problems and failure. As the team's leader, it's up to you to start communicating the team's purpose to members even before they come together for the first time as a team. Because you have already recruited, or your organization has assigned, people to your team, use the time before the first meeting to keep team members informed of the team's purpose. One effective way to pass on this information is through one-on-one meetings with team members. You can also use informal channels such as e-mail bulletins or broadcast voicemails to carry out this task. Make your communications useful. Some of the information new team members will want to have include the date of the first team meeting; travel and lodging information, if necessary; a list of team member names and their responsibilities; and contact information for team members.

Sharing this kind of practical information helps people connect to their new roles as team members, and it also introduces other team members and begins to define their roles. You can also use these pre-meeting communications to explain to team members why they are being brought together and what they are expected to accomplish. By contacting your team early you lay the groundwork for members' feeling responsible for accomplishing a common goal. Achieving that goal, however, requires more than a few introductory e-mails and a meeting itinerary. Successfully setting purpose and direction for your team often hinges on several factors.

Understanding the team's mission. A common purpose for why the team exists and what it has been chartered to do must be clearly communicated to all team members. Developing a mission statement or team vision helps to ensure that team members are all working toward a common end. It establishes the big picture that serves as the basis for setting priorities, making decisions, and allocating resources.

Identifying critical success factors. After the team has clearly defined its mission, it must begin to translate the team vision into action. To take that step during its launch phase, your team should identify the critical factors that will affect its success. Critical success factors are those that the team must accomplish to fulfill its mission. To help your team identify its critical success factors, use a process that solicits input from all team members. Ask the team to think in terms of what it needs to do to be successful. Direct the discussion away from statements of hope, fear, or other intangibles that are difficult to pin down or manage. Ask your team to adhere to a "necessary and sufficient" rule in identifying these factors – each critical success factor should be necessary to the team's mission, not just something that team members desire. Aim for a mix of strategic and tactical statements. Taken together, the critical success factors should be sufficient to achieve the mission.

Creating and owning the team's goals. The amount of energy team members will expend toward reaching goals is to a great extent determined by the degree of participation they have in creating them and determining how they will be accomplished. Goals should be closely aligned to the team's mission. It's important that, whenever possible, members participate in setting team goals. Team members will be more committed to goals they help to create. If goals are mandated from sources outside of the team, give your team members an opportunity to determine how they will accomplish those goals.

Communicating and understanding the team's goals. Team members usually share a general sense of what they are trying to accomplish. However, it is also very common for team members to describe different goals and priorities when asked questions about specific tasks linked to the team's goals. These differences in goal interpretation can lead team members in different directions and may cause conflict and reduce teamwork. Establish clear goals during the launch stage to avert conflict and confusion later during the team's tenure.

Acting upon goals. Challenging and attainable goals help motivate team members. Goals should be well defined, quantified if possible, and specific enough so that members will know when they have succeeded in accomplishing them. For example, setting deadlines or tying other measurements (sales numbers or client contacts, for example) to goals can help your team better organize and use its resources. Establishing milestones also provides your team with a way to assess its progress toward achieving its goals.

Clear Goals Mark High Performance

Gaining clarity about team goals should be a priority in your team's first face-to-face meeting. Teams whose first meeting produces clear goals are likely to be more effective during their tenure. Team members get a chance to learn more about each other during the process and to create an environment of trust that permits discussion and disagreement around high-level strategic issues. That kind of personal investment and authentic dialogue – as opposed to low involvement and polite agreement – is part of what makes teams work.

High-performing Teams	*Low-performing Teams*
The team has a mission statement.	The team does not know why they have come together.
Team members are involved in setting goals and objectives.	Team members have no input on team goals and objectives.
All members understand team goals.	Team goals are unclear.
Members agree on team goals.	Members cannot agree on team goals.
Team goals are challenging and realistically attainable.	Goals are impossible to meet or not challenging enough.

Use the first team meeting to present the purpose of the team to the assembled group. Include relevant background information such as what forces and conditions led up to the decision to launch a team, what business challenges the team will address, and how the team (and the organization) will measure progress toward its goals. Tell the team what the deadlines are for accomplishing its work, what resources are available, and any challenges or constraints it faces. Allow time for discussion after your presentation.

Your presentation and the subsequent discussion provide a basis from which your team can create its own mission statement, from which it will derive its goals. Don't rush this part of the launch. Let team members absorb what they have heard before directing them toward creating their own vision of why the team exists and what it will accomplish. Again, you will want to be aware of the logistics of the first team meeting. If the first meeting takes place in one day, you may want to defer crafting the mission to the second meeting. If the first meeting takes place over two to three days, the mission statement can be created on the second day. Remember, however, that the mission statement should be created relatively early in the team-launch process.

If time is short and you are facing a long agenda for the first team meeting, it can be tempting to simply tell the team what its purpose is and how results will be measured. CCL's experience with teams repeatedly illustrates the value of having teams create their own visions of why they exist and what they aim to accomplish. The process of creating a mission statement inspires and motivates team members, helps them to take ownership of team strategies, and encourages them to take responsibility for their individual contributions. Before the first team meeting ends (or the first day if it is scheduled to run multiple days), distribute a copy of the Mission Statement Worksheet (page 15) to all the members. By creating a mission statement as a group, the team creates a sense of its own uniqueness and a sense of urgency about reaching its goals.

Crafting a Mission Statement

The team leader or sponsor, an external facilitator, or a member of the team experienced in facilitation may lead the group through the process of creating its mission statement. One effective way to get the process going, and which many teams use and many people are familiar with, is brainstorming.

For each question on the Mission Statement Worksheet, use at least one sheet of paper on a flip chart, and have members of the team call out ideas that relate to that question. All suggestions, no matter how wild, should be recorded on the paper. The suggestions should be noted and recorded until the energy level in the room begins to drop.

Post the large sheets of paper around the room, and give everyone the opportunity to go around and look at each sheet. As a group, identify patterns and themes that emerged from the brainstorming exercise, looking for common words and repetition. Discuss how these themes might fit together to form a mission statement.

As a group, draft a mission statement using this strategy: First, ask individual team members to write a mission statement for the team. Next, bring team members together in small groups of three or four and ask them to share their individual statements and create a mission statement from their small group. Finally, bring the entire team together to share the small-group mission statements and to build from those to a single mission statement for the entire team.

If time allows, the group may continue the discussion to arrive at a final, polished version of the statement. Equally effective, a subgroup of the team may be assigned to make revisions and bring the statement back at a later time for approval by the team. Whichever method you choose, make sure that the completed mission statement:

- is understandable, particularly to people who are not members of the team
- refers to specific customer needs the team is trying to meet
- indicates how the team will conduct its work
- reflects challenging but achievable goals
- expresses the mission in a way that will help focus effort, guide decisions, solve problems, and provide inspiration.

Mission Statement Worksheet

As a team member, you can use this worksheet to record your understanding of the team's purpose and your ideas about what you want the team to be like. Use a separate piece of paper if you need more room to capture your thoughts.

What purpose does this team serve?

Who are our customers/clients?

What do they have to gain from our work?

How do we want to be perceived by our customers/clients?

What are our unique capabilities?

What do we want to change?

What gives energy and urgency to our team?

What are our team's core values and how do they relate to the organization's values?

What would we like the legacy of our team to be?

Defining Roles and Responsibilities

Who does what on this team?

According to CCL's research and its work with hundreds of teams, confusion about individual roles and responsibilities is one of the prime factors that can lead to a team's performing below expectations, or worse, failing altogether. For teams to function effectively, each team member must agree to individual roles and responsibilities, and each team member needs to have a clear understanding of what is expected from other team members. Two complementary pieces are necessary:

A clear understanding of individual roles. Most team members assume they know what is expected of other team members, but it's often the case that their assumptions are wrong. When differences exist in the way members perceive their roles and how other members of the team perceive them, misunderstandings and conflict can arise. All team members should understand what they and others are supposed to do to accomplish the team's goal(s). As members of a team work together, they build expectations of one another that are seldom in job descriptions or other organizational documentation. These expectations should be discussed and agreed upon because to a large extent they determine what team members do, how they go about doing it, and what the reactions of other team members are likely to be. When roles and responsibilities are not clearly understood by all team members, there is potential for important tasks to be duplicated or overlooked.

An understanding of individual responsibilities. Roles that overlap can create conflict when two or more members see themselves as responsible for the same task. Also, it's possible that team members will not accept or agree with the role that has been defined for them. (This occurs most frequently when new members of a team do not view their responsibilities in the same way as their predecessors.) Frequent communication among team members about responsibilities is necessary to avoid potential conflict.

Clear Roles and Responsibilities Reduce Conflict and Promote Performance

At the first meeting, provide formal and informal means for team members to get to know one another and to gain insight into what each person brings to the group. For example, you might direct a series of introductions at the beginning of the meeting. Another method, which CCL calls the Home Page (the activity is described on page 18), has proven very beneficial and powerful in helping team members develop an understanding about what they bring to the team. Through these and similar activities, coupled with the introductory communications delivered before the first meeting, team members begin to understand their respective roles and to take responsibility for specific tasks.

High-performing Teams	Low-performing Teams
Roles are clearly defined and do not overlap.	Roles are poorly defined.
Roles are understood and supported by all team members.	Team members engage in power plays for authority. Tasks are left incomplete.
Team members have clearly defined responsibilities for specific tasks.	Team members do not feel responsible for specific tasks and assignments and so those jobs fall through the cracks.
Team members and the team leader are accessible, communicate well, and are available to help each other.	Team members refuse to recognize their interdependence and act as if they are independent sole contributors.

Home Page Activity

This activity takes approximately 20 minutes per person (for example, 8 team members at 20 minutes each requires about 2 hours and 40 minutes) but can be modified to more closely match the time available to your team in its first meeting.

Step 1. Each team member creates a "home page" using a sheet of presentation paper (such as from a flip chart). On the paper each team member writes his or her name at the top, and below that lists the functional responsibilities he or she has in the organization.

Step 2. Every team member walks around the room and reads every home page. Using large "sticky" notes, each person writes a statement in response to the description recorded on each piece of chart paper. The statement should explain what the team member reading the description needs from that team member, whose functional responsibilities are listed on the chart paper, to fulfill his or her role on the team. Team members should sign their sticky notes.

Step 3. After all sticky notes have been attached to the home pages, team members review their individual home pages and write a summary of what is recorded there. Each team member verbally confirms what other teammates need and clarifies what is unclear, setting up meeting times if necessary to work out any conflicts related to team roles and responsibilities.

Option 1. If time is short and the team members already know each other's roles and responsibilities, begin by asking them to write what they need and expect from one another.

Option 2. If more time is available, leave (or attach) the charting papers along the wall and use tape to make connections between team members. Discuss patterns as a group.

No matter what techniques you use during the first team meeting to introduce team members to each other and to their work, there are several key elements that the meeting should address. First, the team should analyze the work it has been asked to do. Second, the team should define shared and individual responsibilities. Third, team members should understand who each team member depends on to get his or her piece of the work accomplished. Finally, team members should understand who is empowered to make decisions – the team as a group, the team leader, or individual members.

Designing Procedures and Practices

> *How do things get done on this team?*

An effective team consistently uses the processes and guidelines it has agreed upon for managing the flow of work, making quality decisions, solving problems, and managing meetings. For members of a team to function well in their efforts to accomplish their goal(s) they must be aware of, agree to, and manage several factors:

How decisions are made. One of the most common challenges facing teams relates to decision making. Most teams don't discuss or reach agreement on the most effective method for making decisions. It's not unusual for two or more members to feel that they are responsible for a specific decision and for a conflict to erupt about who should make it. It's important to see, and crucial for the team leader to make apparent, that this isn't an either/or situation but one in which both parties have a contribution to make. In other instances no one on the team feels responsible for decisions, so no decision is made. The team leader's role in decision making also needs to be clearly stated and understood by the entire team. (For instance, when does the team decide by consensus and when does the team leader make the decision?) The responsibility for decisions and the means by which each team member participates in decisions must be clearly defined so that decisions are of high quality and are accepted by all members.

How to handle communication. Team communication typically falls into one of two camps: either team members do not communicate with each other as much as they should or all information is communicated to every team member. Neither method helps a team's productivity. Effective team communication requires that the team not only manage the quality, quantity, and timing of communication within the team but also have a specific strategy for effectively communicating to individuals and groups with whom the team needs to interact.

How to conduct meetings. If you were to conduct an informal poll of team members you would probably find that a substantial number of them believe that meetings are ineffective, dull, repetitive, too long, too frequent, cover the wrong subjects, are dominated by a few people, or are simply a waste of time. When planning and conducting meetings, team members should always remember what the team is trying to accomplish, what subjects are to be covered in the meeting and in what order they will be addressed, and how those subjects link to the team's objective.

Understanding and agreeing to team norms. As soon as possible, preferably during its first meeting, your team should establish guidelines for what is acceptable and desirable behavior for individuals on the team. These guidelines, or norms, are essential because as a rule team members come from different functional areas of the organization and perhaps from different geographic areas. Each team member arrives with different ideas, assumptions, and expectations. In some organizations, for example, it's normal to interrupt people, tease people, and engage in friendly put-downs. In other departments, business units, or localities, these behaviors are seen as totally out of line. In some organizational cultures it's customary to start meetings late, but in others promptness is the rule. In some workplaces disagreement is welcomed, but in others

Setting Team Norms:
Procedures and Practices for Performance

High-performing teams agree on procedures and on guidelines for how team members should interact with one another and how they should carry out their work. Good communications lie at the heart of a team's procedures, especially when it comes to making decisions and running meetings. Norms lie at the heart of a team's best practices, because these guidelines for behavior allow team members to work together in ways that benefit the group and not just individual contributors.

High-performing Teams	*Low-performing Teams*
Decisions are made by consensus or individually, as needed.	One person makes the decisions.
Meetings are efficient and task-oriented.	Meetings drift from one topic to another without resolution.
Emphasis is on solving problems rather than determining who is to blame.	Considerable effort goes into determining who caused the problem(s).
All members participate in discussions and meetings.	A few team members monopolize discussions.
Minutes of meetings are promptly distributed.	No one agrees on what was accomplished at the meetings.
Members listen well.	There is more side-talk than straight-talk.
There is frequent feedback to individuals regarding performance.	Individual performance is not discussed.
All members are kept informed.	Members do not keep each other informed.
Deadlines and milestones are clearly established and agreed upon.	Deadlines and milestones are ignored or consistently missed.

it's considered rude and hostile. Establishing norms allows your team to create its own culture, with rules of behavior that are agreed upon in advance and accepted by all members. Your team can use the Team Norm Activity on page 24 to explore team members' expectations about working on a team so they can develop some common guidelines for team behavior.

Building Cooperation and Relationships

How do we work together and with others outside the team?

The fourth element of an effective team launch depends heavily on the other three. Cooperation and relationships emerge when team members know what is expected of them and follow guidelines they have mutually agreed on and that help them work together. It's difficult for team members to get along or work well together when there are misunderstandings and disagreements about the team's purpose and direction, roles and responsibilities, or procedures and practices. With a common purpose and direction, clarity about roles and responsibilities, and agreement about processes and practices, the chances for cooperative collaboration are high. To start building cooperation among team members and between your team and the rest of the organization, pay attention to these factors:

Establish a sense of camaraderie. Team members work effectively together when they have established a sense of mutual support, trust, and respect for one another. During the team's launch, preferably at the first meeting, direct introductions in which team members describe their previous experiences on teams (what went well and what needed improvement) and the lessons learned from that work. They might talk about experiences with other projects of a similar nature and their expectations for the current team's work. Team members should state why they were asked to be on the team and what they bring to the team.

Ten Steps to Successful Team Meetings

1. Plan an agenda ahead of time and make sure that people know what they will be working on during the meeting. Detail how much time will be devoted to each subject and who is responsible for each subject.

2. Let team members know in advance what the meeting's purpose is (information giving/receiving, problem solving, or decision making, for example) so they can come prepared to work.

3. Invite the right team members to the meeting. If you know the purpose of the meeting, you can invite the right people with the right information. Not every team member (core team members, extended team members, sponsors/champions, clients/customers) may need to come to every meeting.

4. Monitor the meeting to make sure the team is sticking to the agenda and making progress toward the meeting's purpose.

5. Develop and use meeting guidelines or norms for how the team members will behave with each other.

6. Use an agreed-upon decision-making process when needed. Be aware that all team decisions do not have to be made by consensus.

7. Before the end of the meeting make sure that any decisions, tasks, and actions that need to be followed up are recorded.

8. Obtain commitments for who will do what and when.

9. Use the last 10–15 minutes to debrief how the team meeting went. A simple round-robin answer to the question "How productive was this meeting?" or "Did we stay on the agenda?" or "Did everyone who wanted to speak get a chance to do so?" can help teams develop more effective communication and meeting guidelines that will boost performance.

10. Distribute the minutes of the meeting within one or two days.

Team Norm Activity

This activity can not only draw out what team members think are best practices but also can reveal what kind of actions they think hinder team performance.

Step 1. Ask each member to think of the worst team he or she has served on. Any group counts – a work team, a volunteer group, a sports team, or any other group in which the members were dependent on each other to produce results.

Step 2. Have each team member spend two minutes writing down what made that experience so terrible. Direct them to be as specific as possible about their reasons.

Step 3. Ask team members to share their experiences with the whole group.

Step 4. Ask team members to think of the best team experience they have had. As with the negative experience, each team member should spend two minutes writing down what made the experience so good. Also, as before, encourage team members to share their experiences with the whole team.

Step 5. With these comments in mind, discuss as a group what makes for a good and a bad team experience.

Step 6. Ask team members to suggest behaviors that would make serving on the current team a positive experience and contribute to the team's success. Record these suggestions on a large sheet of paper that all team members can view.

Step 7. Discuss the suggestions as a group and decide as a group which ones the team agrees it can support and adhere to.

Step 8. Transfer the list to a form that you can send to all team members after the meeting (in an e-mail message, for example, or posted on the company's intranet) so they can recall and refer to them. Your team may choose to post its list of norms in its regular meeting room for quick reference.

Manage conflicts. Even with these pieces in place, relationships inside of a team can become strained. Conflicts can occur because of differences in personalities and/or communication styles. They can also result from confusion about purpose and direction, roles and responsibilities, or procedures and practices. Energy that is siphoned off by bad feelings, attitudes, or confusion is unavailable for accomplishing the team's goal(s). Open and honest communication can help team members deal constructively with these issues as they arise. Members need ways to resolve conflicts and to assure that good working relationships are developed and maintained. The team should develop such means as part of its procedures and practices. Developing clear guidelines and getting the endorsement of the team is key to circumventing or resolving such conflicts.

Review and monitor external relationships. When you formed your team you identified the key relationships between the team and its stakeholders inside and outside the organization and worked out processes for developing and maintaining them. It's helpful to reexamine those relationships when you launch your team. Changes in vendors and suppliers, new information about customers, restructuring within the company, turnover of some key people, and other shifts can all test your team's ability to adapt and perform effectively. This is also the time to think more specifically about whom the team will need help and support from, how your team might extend into the territory of other groups, and whom it needs to keep apprised of its work. Review the information/resources your team will need from others. Think about what the organization expects from your team and the chances that those expectations will shift and require building new key relationships. Prepare your team for a successful launch by knowing (and sharing with team members) what groups and which individuals the team must productively interact with and where cooperative relationships must be maintained and nurtured.

Working Together to Build Performance

Working together as a team doesn't mean setting aside personal differences. It means understanding those differences and adapting to them as they fit within the procedures and practices to which the team has agreed. A tool like the "Getting to Know You" Icebreaker (page 27) is useful for helping team members gain a better understanding and appreciation of their colleagues' abilities and interests. As a team leader you will need to help your team find the common ground from which it can solve conflicts, manage internal and external relationships, and generate its highest performance.

High-performing Teams	*Low-performing Teams*
There is team spirit and pride.	Members do not identify with the team.
There is tolerance for conflict and an emphasis on resolution.	There is covert conflict between team members.
Conflict is acknowledged and openly discussed.	Conflict is avoided or not dealt with constructively.
Team members are open and friendly with one another.	Relationships are competitive.
Team members support each other.	Team members are defensive and not supportive of one another.

Discuss the relationship between the team and its leader. Leadership style affects a team's communication, cooperation, decision making, and work processes. Some effective team leaders are authoritarian and others are more participative. As a team leader you should be aware of the style you tend to use and the impact that style may have on your team's effectiveness. You aren't locked into any one style; in fact, some of the most effective team leaders are able to adapt their style of leadership to fit different situations. If you have helped your team create a supportive environment that is open to feedback from all members, then you can seek feedback regarding how leadership style contributes to or detracts from the team's effectiveness. If no leader has been designated, teams need to identify key leadership responsibilities and determine how they will be carried out.

"Getting to Know You" Icebreaker

Teams work better when members appreciate one another for more than their business savvy and organizational skills. Here's an exercise that helps team members get to know their teammates personally: Pair up with a partner and describe two physical attributes you like about yourself, two personality qualities you like about yourself, and one talent or skill you like about yourself. Then have your partner do the same.

Countdown to Team Success

For your team to reach its goals, every team member has to know the team's mission, be able to recognize success, and be willing to work with other team members to achieve the common goal. Establishing the team's purpose and direction during its launch is the first and most fundamental factor of team effectiveness. If team members disagree on why they are together and what they are trying to accomplish, problems will inevitably arise to negatively affect the team's performance.

Establishing purpose and direction provides a context for roles and responsibilities to be understood and accepted. When these keys are developed during the team's launch, team members can better grasp the significance of why they and the others are being expected to perform certain tasks. They can see how doing what is expected will contribute to achieving the team's goal(s).

Once team members have a clear understanding of what they are supposed to do, procedures and practices can help them shape the best way of working together to coordinate their activities.

As the team's leader you are in a powerful position to influence whether your team realizes its potential. Team members need to feel inspired by the opportunity and confident that they will have the resources and support needed for success. They need to have positive feelings about the people they will depend on to accomplish the team's mission. A strong launch sets a clear direction, an inspiring challenge, and a cooperative spirit that will enable your team to achieve its full potential.

Suggested Readings

Duarte, D. L., & Snyder, N. T. (1999). *Mastering virtual teams: Strategies, tools, and techniques that succeed.* San Francisco: Jossey-Bass.

Dyer, W. G. (1995). *Team building, current issues and new alternatives* (3rd ed.). Reading, MA: Addison-Wesley.

Kanaga, K., & Kossler, M. E. (2001). *How to form a team: Five keys to high performance.* Greensboro, NC: Center for Creative Leadership.

Katzenbach, J. R., & Smith, D. K. (1993). *The wisdom of teams.* Boston, MA: Harvard Business School Press.

Kossler, M. E., & Kanaga, K. (2001). *Do you really need a team?* Greensboro, NC: Center for Creative Leadership.

Rayner, S. R. (1996). *Team traps: Survival stories and lessons from team disasters, near-misses, mishaps, and other near-death experiences.* New York: John Wiley & Sons.

Rubin, I. M., Plovnik, M. S., & Fry, R. E. (1978). *Task-oriented team development.* New York: McGraw-Hill.

Sessa, V. I., Hansen, M. C., Prestridge, S., & Kossler, M. E. (1999). *Geographically dispersed teams: An annotated bibliography.* Greensboro, NC: Center for Creative Leadership.

Background

Since the mid-1980s, the Center for Creative Leadership (CCL) has worked with many organizations and teams through its educational initiatives. The goal of these initiatives is to help participants develop team management skills through a proven process that combines personal assessment, feedback from the workplace, and experience with practical, team-oriented applications. These developmental experiences provide research-based information about how high-performance teams work; honest appraisals of existing teams' strengths and weaknesses; and proven approaches for turning average performers into a highly effective team. It covers such issues as selecting team members, launching teams effectively, bridging cross-cultural differences in teams, and resolving team conflict. Through training programs, research, and custom interventions, CCL continues to provide a hands-on learning experience for team leaders that emphasizes a range of practical tools and strategies for enhancing the performance of any team.

In addition to providing these team-oriented educational programs and customized interventions, in 1996 CCL launched a research project on the work and performance of geographically dispersed teams. Since 1997, CCL faculty members have presented their findings and analyses at conferences and through publications. That research helps to further inform CCL's classroom content. CCL continues its work with clients and with other scholars to further develop its understanding of teams – how they can be led more effectively, how they can best achieve organizational goals, and how they can be created and maintained for improved results. CCL seeks to pass that understanding on to team leaders and their organizations so teams can meet or surpass performance expectations.

Key Point Summary

Teams can produce innovative solutions to complex problems, enabling organizations to be faster, more responsive, more competitive, and more successful in meeting their missions. But these kinds of results aren't guaranteed. It's not always easy for teams to deliver high performance. A good start is crucial to ensuring that your team will function successfully.

To launch a team toward success, managers and team leaders should pay attention to four critical points: setting purpose and direction, defining roles and responsibilities, designing procedures and practices, and building cooperation and relationships. Understanding and implementing these elements are key to a successful launch and, in the end, essential to a team's achieving the organization's goals.

Setting purpose and direction hinges on your team's understanding its mission, creating its goals, and being able to act upon its goals. Defining roles and responsibilities requires team members to have a clear understanding of what they contribute to the team and what the team is asking of them. Designing procedures and practices means paying attention to how decisions are made on your team, working out how to handle team communication, and having the team understand and agree to team norms. Building cooperation and relationships during the team launch means establishing a sense of camaraderie, managing conflicts, reviewing and monitoring external relationships, identifying critical success factors, and defining the relationship between the team and its leader.

Team members need to feel inspired by the opportunity and confident that they will have the resources and support needed for success. A strong launch sets a clear direction, an inspiring challenge, and a cooperative spirit that will enable your team to serve the organization with exceptional performance.

Related Publications

DO YOU REALLY NEED A TEAM?

Teams are expensive and time consuming to launch, and leading a team is a full-time job. Teams can do a great job of addressing complex problems and issues that affect many parts of the organization and its people. But for decisions that must be reached . quickly, or when a diversity of perspectives is not needed, smaller and more easily managed work units are a better choice. Before launching a team, analyze the task at hand to make sure that a team is really what you need to get the job done.

HOW TO FORM A TEAM: FIVE KEYS TO HIGH PERFORMANCE

If you are a department head or project manager, or if you are the senior-level champion or sponsor of a proposed team, you need to understand the five factors critical to building effective teams and how to use those factors to lay the groundwork for successful teams.

HOW TO LAUNCH A TEAM: START RIGHT FOR SUCCESS

Getting your team off on the right foot is critical to its success. To launch a team so that it increases its chance of success, managers and team leaders should pay attention to four critical points: setting purpose and direction, defining roles and responsibilities, designing procedures and practices, and building cooperation and relationships. Understanding and implementing these elements is key to helping your team accomplish its mission.

LEADING DISPERSED TEAMS

Dispersed teams are a necessary, strategic work unit in a world that continues to grow more interconnected every day. Guiding them to their full potential is a difficult challenge for even the most seasoned team leader. Solving potential communication problems and devising processes for making decisions and managing conflict are key leadership challenges for those managers. Creating an effective first-time meeting and securing organizational support are critical to success.

MAINTAINING TEAM PERFORMANCE

Team success isn't inevitable. Leaders who monitor and maintain their team so that it operates at peak efficiency can ensure that it successfully achieves its goal. By assessing their team's effort, knowledge and skills, tactics, and group dynamics, leaders can diagnose problems and make corrections to bring the team back on track.

Purchase our **TEAMS GUIDEBOOK PACKAGE** and receive the above five titles at a significant savings. See below for ordering information.

Ordering Information

FOR MORE INFORMATION, TO ORDER OTHER IDEAS INTO ACTION GUIDEBOOKS, OR TO FIND OUT ABOUT BULK-ORDER DISCOUNTS, PLEASE CONTACT US BY PHONE AT 336-545-2810 OR VISIT OUR ONLINE BOOKSTORE AT WWW.CCL.ORG/ GUIDEBOOKS. PREPAYMENT IS REQUIRED FOR ALL ORDERS UNDER $100.